At the Shore

Story by Suzanne Barchers
Illustrated by Anthony Lewis
Designed and Produced by Six Red Marbles

"Oh Dad," says Tom. "Can we go to the beach for sand, shade, and sun?"

"Yes!" says Dad. "We could sail on a ship. It would be lots of fun."

"First we'll walk to the dock. Then we'll board a ship."

"You will get your wish to go on an exciting trip."

Winds push the ship. Winds push them some more.

Sails shift and shake and push the ship past the shore.

The fish in the sea flash fins in the sun.

Fish swish by the ship and jump one by one.

"It is time for a rest," says Mom. "We can read in the shade."

Fran says, "Let's sit on the sand and sip lemonade."

Crash! The waves smash on the seashore.

The children dash away, then dash back for more.

Fran finds a shell. She will brush off the sand.

Look at the shell shine in Fran's hand.

Tom finds a shell. "Nate, come and see!"

"See the shell's shape? What kind of shell can it be?"

"This is shaped like a star," says Nate. "Can we make a wish?"

"No, it is not in the sky," says Tom. "It's a starfish!"

The tide rushes in. The tide rushes out.

They get wet. They all shake and shout.

Now Mom wants to shop for a dish that holds fish.

Tom tags along and shops for his wish.

 They pack up the shells and shut the trash. They brush off the sand and head home in a flash.

Let's learn some more!